Special thanks to the North Branch School District staff and students for participating in the creation of Set 2 of the That's Life Literature Series.

PURPOSE
Learn strategies for finding places you want to go!

WORDS TO KNOW

- **address**
  numbers that identify a location

- **directions**
  information on how to locate a place

- **information center**
  a place that offers help to get to where you want to go

- **landmark**
  an object that marks a location

- **map**
  a representation usually on a flat surface of a location or area

- **phone book**
  a book containing addresses and phone numbers of homes and businesses

THINGS TO THINK ABOUT

Teenagers go places for many different reasons. For example, they go to the movies for entertainment, fast food restaurants for meals, friends' houses to visit, the mall to buy clothing and the beach to swim.

1. When you go somewhere, how do you get there?
2. Who do you ask for help?
3. Where is the last place you went? Why did you go there? How did you get there?

TOPIC:
Finding One's Way

APPROACH:
Teen Advice

AUDIENCE:
Secondary School Special Education Students

AbleNet, Inc.
Mpls./St.Paul, MN USA
Toll Free: 1-800-322-0956 (US and Canada only)
Internet: www.ablenetinc.com

All rights reserved. No part of this book may be reproduced or transmitted in any form or by any means, electronic or mechanical, including photocopying, recording or by any information storage and retrieval system without permission from the publisher.

You're There!

A Teen's Guide to Going Places

By Marybeth Lorbiecki • Design by David Bradley
Photography by Jim Gallop

Let's get going!

That's Life! Literature Series
Developing Life Skills through teen advice, real-life stories, word play, and social games.

Set 2: Going Places Theme - Book 1
© AbleNet, Inc. * Minneapolis/St. Paul, Minnesota

Ever make plans with a friend to meet you somewhere and then you don't know how to get there?

"Use white pages for people's homes. Use the yellow pages for places like movie theaters, shops, and pizza parlors."

You can ask someone to draw a map -- those are the coolest!

10.

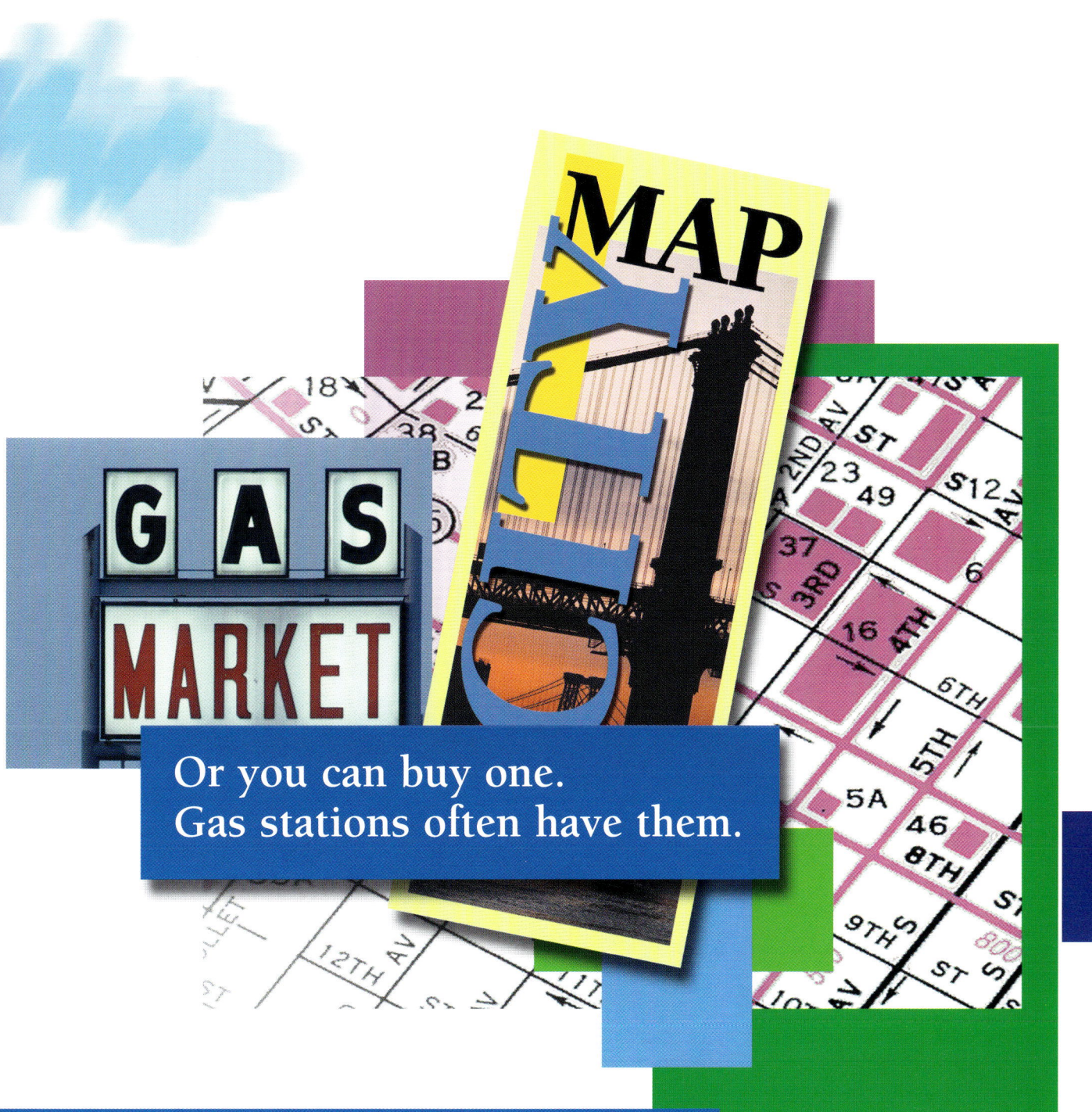

Or you can buy one.
Gas stations often have them.

Some schools, buildings, and cities have information centers.

You can also find maps on your computer. The Internet has map sites.

13.

15.

TALKING POINTS

- What ways in this book have you used to find a place?
- What ways would you like to learn?
- If you were going to tell someone how to get to your home, what landmarks would you mention?
- What landmarks would you mention when telling someone how to get to school, the mall, the library and another location in your community?

CREATIVE WAYS TO USE THIS BOOK

- Calling Directory Assistance is a great way to find a phone number of a place you want to go. Practice calling Directory Assistance and writing down the information. Then call the place for directions.
- Think about a place that you like to go and describe how you get there.
- List the different ways that you have learned to find out the address of a place you want to go?

Use the *That's Life! Literature Series* with the AbleNet BookWorm™ Literacy Tool:

The Bookworm Literacy Tool makes almost any book into a "talking book." Now it's easy for all students to participate in meaningful literacy experiences! Each book in the set has preprinted sticker locations that make it fast and easy to use with the BookWorm. Prerecorded modules are also available for each set of books in the series. Visit www.ablenetinc.com for more information.

BookWorm™ Literacy Tool